# Unseen Shadows: Inside the Realm of RAW

## Table of Contents

# Chapter 12: Legacy of Excellence - Shaping the Future of RAW

## Chapter 1: Inception and Genesis

Deep within the corridors of power, during the tumultuous days of 1968, India's Prime Minister, Indira Gandhi, recognized the need for a dedicated intelligence agency. The world around her was changing rapidly, and national security required an organization that could effectively navigate the treacherous waters of global politics. Thus, RAW came into being, shrouded in secrecy, with a mission to safeguard India's interests at home and abroad.

As the first chapter of RAW's tale unfolds, it reveals the intricate web of events that led to its inception. Indira Gandhi handpicked Rameshwar Nath Kao, a seasoned intelligence officer, to shape and lead the fledgling agency. Kao was a visionary who possessed an unparalleled understanding of the intelligence landscape. His vision extended beyond traditional intelligence gathering, focusing on covert operations and strategic analysis.

With Kao at the helm, a team of brilliant minds was assembled, drawn from various sectors of Indian society. These individuals shared a deep commitment to the nation and possessed unique skills that would help RAW establish its foothold in the world of intelligence. Together, they formed the backbone of an organization that would become synonymous with courage, stealth, and unwavering dedication.

RAW's early years were fraught with challenges. The agency had to contend with limited resources, an evolving geopolitical landscape, and the weighty task of building a robust intelligence network from scratch. In the face of these obstacles, Kao's leadership and the commitment of his team became the driving force behind RAW's growth.

This chapter explores the agency's initial struggles and triumphs as RAW delved into the realm of intelligence gathering, counterintelligence, and covert operations. It sheds light on RAW's early operations, including its instrumental role in the liberation of Bangladesh in 1971—a defining moment that showcased the agency's capability to shape history.

As RAW embarked on its journey, it swiftly garnered a reputation for its ability to adapt to changing circumstances, find innovative solutions to complex problems, and protect national interests with precision. Its network of agents, informants, and sources spanned the globe, collecting information vital to India's security. RAW's officers infiltrated foreign organizations, established networks of spies, and penetrated the depths of international terrorist organizations—all in service of their sacred duty.

The genesis of RAW was marked by secrecy, sacrifice, and an unyielding commitment to the nation. With each passing day, the organization grew stronger, honing its skills and expanding its reach. However, little did the world know that RAW's true potential and the depth of its operations remained hidden beneath the surface, obscured by the shadows in which it thrived.

Chapter 1 of "Unseen Shadows: Inside the Realm of RAW" lays the foundation for the journey that lies ahead. It is a glimpse into the agency's inception, its early challenges, and the men and women who devoted their lives to serving their country in silence. The subsequent chapters will unveil the untold stories of RAW's covert operations, its pivotal role in shaping Indian foreign policy, and the legends that emerged from the shadows to become unsung heroes.

Join us as we delve deeper into the intriguing world of RAW, where reality is often stranger than fiction, and where secrets are guarded with unwavering loyalty. Brace yourself for a journey that will take you from the corridors of power to the heart of danger, revealing the enigmatic operations and the remarkable individuals who make up the tapestry of India's premier intelligence agency.

## Chapter 2: Operation Janus - A Test of Fire

India's northern borders had always been a matter of strategic importance, and the treacherous terrains of the Himalayas posed unique challenges for national security. It was amidst these challenging circumstances that Operation Janus took shape—an endeavor designed to secure vital intelligence on enemy movements in the region.

The origins of Operation Janus can be traced back to the early 1980s when tensions between India and its neighboring country reached a boiling point. RAW's intelligence assessments indicated an imminent threat to the country's security, necessitating a bold and decisive response. Under the guidance of their seasoned leaders, RAW operatives meticulously planned the operation, leaving no room for error.

The objective was clear—to infiltrate deep into enemy territory, gather critical information, and relay it back to the Indian defense forces. However, the path to success was riddled with dangers. The operatives had to navigate icy mountain passes, evade enemy patrols, and operate in extreme weather conditions. The margin for error was razor-thin, and the consequences of failure could be catastrophic.

RAW's specialized training academies had prepared the operatives for this very moment. Their physical endurance, combat skills, and mastery of covert techniques would be put to the ultimate test. With each step they took, the operatives knew that their survival relied not only on their individual prowess but also on their ability to function as a cohesive unit, trusting one another with their lives.

Operation Janus unfolded in the dead of night, as a team of highly trained commandos silently crossed the border, disappearing into the abyss of enemy territory. For weeks, they operated in the shadows, gathering intelligence, infiltrating enemy installations, and monitoring troop movements. Their success hinged on their ability to remain undetected—a high-stakes game of cat and mouse where a single misstep could shatter the mission and compromise national security.

The challenges were relentless. RAW operatives faced hostile encounters with enemy forces, encountered treacherous weather conditions, and navigated unfamiliar terrain. They relied on their wits, ingenuity, and the unwavering support of their comrades to stay one step ahead of their adversaries. The operation demanded not only physical resilience but also mental fortitude, as the operatives constantly balanced on the tightrope between triumph and tragedy.

As the days turned into weeks, Operation Janus reached a critical juncture. The operatives had collected a trove of valuable information, which, if utilized effectively, could tilt the balance in India's favor. However, extracting themselves from enemy territory would prove just as challenging as their infiltration. The risk of discovery grew exponentially with each passing hour, forcing them to rely on their training, resourcefulness, and a touch of luck.

Chapter 2 of "Unseen Shadows: Inside the Realm of RAW" takes you deep into the heart of Operation Janus—a mission that encapsulated the indomitable spirit of RAW. It unveils the immense risks undertaken by the operatives, the sacrifices made in the pursuit of national security, and the untold stories that emerged from the crucible of battle.

Join us as we traverse the treacherous mountains, witness the audacity of RAW's operatives, and discover the power of unwavering determination in the face of adversity. In the chapters to come, we will unravel more of RAW's covert operations, delve into the intricacies of intelligence gathering, and shine a light on the dedicated men and women who remain the unsung heroes of India's intelligence community.

## Chapter 3: Shadows of Espionage - The Great Game Unveiled

Intelligence agencies across the globe engage in a perpetual dance, a game where nations vie for dominance, influence, and the protection of their interests. India, too, has been an active participant in this intricate web of espionage, often referred to as the "Great Game." As RAW evolved and grew in strength, it stepped onto the global stage, forging alliances, gathering intelligence, and navigating the murky waters of international politics.

The early years of RAW saw the agency establishing a robust network of informants and agents across key regions of interest. From the bustling streets of Kabul to the vibrant bazaars of Tehran, RAW's operatives worked tirelessly to collect vital information on regional dynamics, counterterrorism efforts, and the ever-shifting geopolitical landscape.

One of RAW's notable successes in this era was its pivotal role in unraveling a notorious spy network operating within India. This network, with deep-rooted connections to hostile nations, posed a significant threat to India's security. RAW's intelligence officers, armed with determination and a relentless pursuit of truth, meticulously uncovered the network's operations, leading to the arrest and subsequent dismantling of this clandestine apparatus.

As RAW's reputation grew, it found itself engaging in a delicate dance with other intelligence agencies. The game of espionage demanded not only vigilance but also the cultivation of strategic alliances with like-minded nations. RAW forged partnerships with intelligence agencies of friendly nations, exchanging critical information and expertise, and collectively combating transnational threats.

RAW's international collaborations extended beyond mere intelligence sharing. It often found itself acting as a conduit, facilitating diplomatic negotiations, and offering backchannel communication between nations. In the turbulent landscape of international relations, RAW emerged as a trusted mediator, providing valuable insights and bridging gaps that could have otherwise led to escalating tensions.

The Great Game, however, is a realm of shifting allegiances and hidden agendas. As RAW navigated the complex world of international intelligence, it encountered instances where trust was misplaced and allies turned into adversaries. RAW's officers became experts in deciphering the nuances of diplomacy, reading between the lines, and identifying the true intentions of foreign powers.

Chapter 3 of "Unseen Shadows: Inside the Realm of RAW" unravels the intricate threads of the Great Game, where the agency's operatives became master manipulators, blending in with the shadows, and outmaneuvering their opponents. It reveals the delicate balance RAW had to maintain between cooperation and suspicion, constantly adapting its strategies to protect national interests and ensure the safety of its agents in the field.

Join us as we dive deeper into the clandestine world of international espionage, where alliances are forged in secrecy, trust is a luxury, and every move carries profound consequences. In the forthcoming chapters, we will uncover more covert operations, shed light on the challenges faced by RAW's operatives, and explore the enduring legacy of India's premier intelligence agency.

## Chapter 4: The Trail of Shadows - Counterterrorism and National Security

The shockwaves of the 9/11 terrorist attacks reverberated across the globe, awakening nations to the urgent need for robust counterterrorism efforts. India found itself thrust into the forefront of this battle, facing the persistent threat of terrorism emanating from both within and beyond its borders. RAW rose to the challenge, taking up the mantle of defending the nation against this evolving menace.

As the chapter unfolds, we witness RAW's transformation into a formidable force against terrorism. The agency established specialized counterterrorism units, equipped with cutting-edge technology and a deep understanding of the complexities of the threat landscape. These units became the vanguard of India's counterterrorism efforts, tirelessly working to dismantle terrorist networks, neutralize threats, and prevent future attacks.

RAW's counterterrorism operations extended beyond Indian soil. The agency collaborated closely with international partners, sharing intelligence, coordinating efforts, and participating in joint operations to combat transnational terrorist organizations. It played a vital role in unraveling the intricate financing networks that sustained terrorist activities, choking their funding and disrupting their operations.

In the pursuit of counterterrorism, RAW's operatives had to immerse themselves in the shadows, infiltrating extremist organizations, and gathering intelligence from the heart of the beast. Their dedication, courage, and unwavering commitment to the cause often meant placing their lives on the line, operating in dangerous territories, and working undercover to gain critical insights into terrorist activities.

One such operation that showcased RAW's prowess was the dismantling of a major terrorist cell plotting to carry out a series of coordinated attacks in multiple Indian cities. RAW's intelligence apparatus, backed by meticulous planning and swift execution, thwarted the plans and apprehended the key operatives, preventing a catastrophe that could have had far-reaching consequences.

RAW's counterterrorism efforts also encompassed proactive measures such as intelligence sharing and capacity-building with partner nations. The agency recognized the importance of addressing the root causes of terrorism, engaging in initiatives to counter radicalization, and collaborating with regional partners to foster stability and peace.

Chapter 4 of "Unseen Shadows: Inside the Realm of RAW" sheds light on the intricate dance between RAW and the forces of terror. It explores the challenges faced by the agency, from the relentless pursuit of intelligence to the ever-present risk of infiltration and betrayal. It highlights the dedication and sacrifice of RAW's operatives, who work tirelessly in the shadows to ensure the safety and security of the nation.

Join us as we venture deeper into the realm of counterterrorism, where the stakes are high, the enemy is cunning, and the battle for national security is fought on multiple fronts. In the upcoming chapters, we will delve into the covert operations, intelligence breakthroughs, and the relentless pursuit of justice that define RAW's unwavering commitment to protecting India from the scourge of terrorism.

## Chapter 5: Eyes in the Dark - Technological Frontiers of Intelligence

In an era where information flows freely across digital networks and secrets are increasingly harder to keep, RAW understood the critical role that technology played in intelligence operations. As the agency continued to evolve, it actively embraced the technological frontiers to enhance its capabilities, enabling it to adapt to the ever-changing landscape of intelligence.

This chapter unravels the advancements that RAW made in harnessing technology to its advantage. The agency invested in state-of-the-art surveillance systems, satellite imaging, and cyber intelligence capabilities, ushering in a new era of intelligence gathering. It utilized cutting-edge tools to intercept communications, monitor online activities, and track the movements of individuals and organizations of interest.

One notable advancement that played a pivotal role in RAW's operations was the development of its own proprietary intelligence analysis software. This powerful tool allowed the agency to process vast amounts of data, identify patterns, and extract actionable intelligence efficiently. The software's algorithms, combined with the expertise of RAW's analysts, enabled the agency to uncover critical insights that might have otherwise remained hidden.

Furthermore, RAW leveraged its expertise in cyber intelligence, recognizing the growing significance of the digital realm as both a target and a source of intelligence. The agency established dedicated teams of cyber experts, skilled in identifying and countering cyber threats, conducting cyber espionage, and safeguarding critical infrastructure from cyber attacks. RAW's cyber warriors engaged in a constant battle on the virtual battleground, defending national interests and staying one step ahead of the adversaries.

The advent of social media and the proliferation of online platforms presented both opportunities and challenges for intelligence agencies. RAW recognized the power of these platforms as tools for propaganda, recruitment, and communication for hostile entities. The agency adeptly navigated the virtual landscape, monitoring extremist activities, infiltrating online networks, and countering the dissemination of misinformation.

In addition to its focus on the digital realm, RAW continued to explore advancements in other domains as well. It harnessed the potential of unmanned aerial vehicles (UAVs) for surveillance and reconnaissance, providing critical intelligence in remote and hostile regions. It also developed sophisticated listening devices, concealed cameras, and other covert tools that enabled operatives to gather intelligence discreetly and undetected.

Chapter 5 of "Unseen Shadows: Inside the Realm of RAW" reveals how technology became an indispensable ally of the agency, empowering its operatives with unprecedented capabilities. It explores the challenges and ethical considerations that accompanied these advancements, as well as the ongoing race to stay ahead in the ever-competitive technological landscape.

Join us as we embark on a journey into the world of cutting-edge intelligence technology, where innovation and adaptation form the bedrock of success. In the upcoming chapters, we will delve deeper into the covert operations enabled by technology, the ethical dilemmas faced by intelligence agencies, and the relentless pursuit of truth and security in the digital age.

## Chapter 6: The Veiled Wars - Covert Operations Beyond Borders

As RAW's reputation and capabilities grew, the agency found itself increasingly involved in covert operations beyond the borders of India. These operations were carried out in the pursuit of national security, countering threats to India's interests, and influencing events in regions of strategic importance.

In this chapter, we explore the clandestine world of RAW's cross-border operations, where secrecy, deception, and precision were paramount. RAW's operatives, often working under deep cover, infiltrated foreign territories, operated within hostile environments, and executed high-risk missions with the utmost precision.

One notable operation that exemplifies RAW's covert capabilities was the disruption of a transnational terrorist network with deep-rooted connections across South Asia. RAW's operatives, leveraging their networks of informants and covert assets, meticulously gathered intelligence, identified key operatives, and coordinated with international partners to dismantle the network from within. The operation dealt a severe blow to the infrastructure of terrorism, safeguarding not only India but also the stability of the entire region.

RAW's reach extended beyond counterterrorism operations. The agency engaged in covert diplomacy, utilizing backchannels and intermediaries to influence political developments, mediate conflicts, and shape outcomes favorable to India. RAW's operatives played key roles in negotiating sensitive agreements, fostering diplomatic relationships, and mitigating tensions between nations. Their efforts often operated in the shadows, hidden from public view but with far-reaching implications.

Another aspect of RAW's cross-border operations involved supporting movements for self-determination and liberation. The agency clandestinely aided oppressed groups seeking independence or fighting for their rights, aligning with India's commitment to justice and human rights. RAW's operatives provided training, logistical support, and strategic guidance to these movements, striking a delicate balance between advancing India's interests and respecting international norms.

These covert operations, however, were not without risks. RAW's operatives operated in a world where betrayal lurked at every corner, where the lines between friend and foe were often blurred. The agency faced threats from rival intelligence agencies, double agents, and adversaries seeking to exploit vulnerabilities. RAW's ability to safeguard its operations, protect its assets, and maintain the trust of its partners was essential to its success.

Chapter 6 of "Unseen Shadows: Inside the Realm of RAW" peels back the layers of secrecy surrounding RAW's cross-border covert operations. It unveils the intricate strategies, the risks undertaken, and the triumphs achieved in the pursuit of India's national security objectives. It is a testament to the agency's audacity, adaptability, and unwavering commitment to safeguarding India's interests on the global stage.

Join us as we uncover the untold stories of RAW's covert operations beyond borders, where every mission is a delicate dance of shadows, every decision a calculated risk, and every success a testament to the dedication and bravery of those who serve in the name of India's security. In the upcoming chapters, we will explore more covert operations, delve into the complexities of intelligence warfare, and shed light on the individuals who carry out these clandestine missions with unwavering resolve.

## Chapter 7: The Unsung Heroes - RAW's Operatives in the Field

The world of intelligence is a realm of shadows, where the unsung heroes of agencies like RAW undertake clandestine missions that shape the course of events. These operatives embody the spirit of dedication, selflessness, and unwavering commitment to protecting their nation. This chapter delves into their world, uncovering their training, experiences, and the sacrifices they willingly make to keep their country safe.

RAW's operatives undergo rigorous training, preparing them for the arduous challenges they will face in the field. Their training is comprehensive, covering a diverse range of skills, including intelligence gathering, surveillance techniques, hand-to-hand combat, language proficiency, and the art of disguise. They are trained to adapt to any situation, to blend seamlessly into different environments, and to operate under extreme pressure with resilience and composure.

Once in the field, these operatives work in a constant state of vigilance, their identities concealed, and their true allegiance known only to a select few. They operate with an acute awareness of the risks they face, navigating a world where trust is a luxury and betrayal can be fatal. They rely on their instincts, training, and the support of their fellow operatives to overcome obstacles and achieve their objectives.

Their work is marked by long periods away from loved ones, operating in unfamiliar territories, and enduring physical and mental strain. The sacrifices they make are significant, often going unrecognized and unacknowledged. They lead double lives, balancing the demands of their covert work with the need for normalcy when they return home, guarding their secrets and shouldering the weight of their experiences alone.

RAW's operatives possess a unique blend of courage, resourcefulness, and adaptability. They are adept at operating in diverse cultural contexts, immersing themselves in foreign societies, and developing relationships with individuals who can provide valuable intelligence. Their ability to build trust and establish networks of sources is paramount to their success.

In this chapter, we uncover the stories of a few such operatives who have made significant contributions to RAW's operations. We witness their resilience in the face of adversity, their unwavering loyalty to their country, and their determination to protect the nation from threats that lurk in the shadows.

Their stories reveal the human side of intelligence work—the toll it takes on their personal lives, the psychological impact of their experiences, and the challenges they face in readjusting to civilian life. They are ordinary individuals who have chosen an extraordinary path, driven by a deep sense of duty and a commitment to making a difference.

Chapter 7 of "Unseen Shadows: Inside the Realm of RAW" pays tribute to these unsung heroes, shining a light on their sacrifices and resilience. It is a reminder that behind every intelligence success, there are individuals who silently carry the weight of their nation's security on their shoulders.

Join us as we delve deeper into the world of RAW's operatives in the field, where courage, dedication, and selflessness intersect. In the forthcoming chapters, we will continue to unveil the stories of these remarkable individuals, their triumphs, their struggles, and the impact they have on the intricate tapestry of India's intelligence community.

## Chapter 8: The Pursuit of Justice - RAW's Role in Uncovering Global Threats

RAW's mandate extends beyond the borders of India, encompassing the responsibility to protect the global community from the scourge of transnational threats. As the world grapples with the challenges posed by terrorism, organized crime, and the proliferation of weapons of mass destruction, RAW plays a vital role in uncovering these threats and spearheading efforts to bring the perpetrators to justice.

This chapter explores RAW's tireless pursuit of justice on the global stage. The agency's intelligence gathering capabilities, extensive network of sources, and collaborations with international partners enable it to uncover intricate networks that span continents. RAW's operatives work alongside their counterparts from other intelligence agencies, sharing intelligence, coordinating operations, and conducting joint investigations to dismantle these global threats at their roots.

One significant area of RAW's involvement is countering the proliferation of weapons of mass destruction (WMDs). RAW's intelligence apparatus closely monitors the movements of extremist groups, rogue nations, and illicit networks involved in the acquisition, development, and dissemination of WMD-related technologies. Through its vigilant efforts, RAW has contributed to thwarting several attempts to proliferate such dangerous weapons, safeguarding global security and stability.

RAW's role in combating organized crime and drug trafficking cannot be underestimated. The agency's intelligence capabilities provide valuable insights into the operations of transnational criminal organizations involved in drug trafficking, money laundering, and human trafficking. RAW's collaboration with international law enforcement agencies allows for the disruption of these criminal networks, leading to arrests, seizures, and the dismantling of their illicit enterprises.

Moreover, RAW plays an active role in uncovering and countering the activities of extremist organizations and terrorist networks that pose a global threat. Its operatives work tirelessly to gather intelligence on these groups, infiltrate their ranks, and disrupt their operations. Through strategic partnerships with other intelligence agencies and international efforts, RAW's contributions aid in preventing acts of terror and protecting innocent lives worldwide.

RAW's pursuit of justice extends to advocating for human rights and supporting causes aligned with freedom and democracy. The agency lends its expertise to aid nations grappling with political instability, assisting in conflict resolution, and facilitating humanitarian efforts. RAW's intelligence assessments and recommendations inform the decision-making processes of Indian policymakers and international bodies alike, fostering a safer and more just world.

Chapter 8 of "Unseen Shadows: Inside the Realm of RAW" sheds light on RAW's global footprint and its vital role in uncovering and confronting global threats. It showcases the agency's commitment to justice, cooperation, and a safer world for all. RAW's endeavors transcend national boundaries as it stands at the forefront of the fight against terror, proliferation, and organized crime.

Join us as we delve into the intricacies of RAW's contributions to global security, witness its collaborations with international partners, and uncover the relentless pursuit of justice that defines the agency's ethos. In the upcoming chapters, we will continue to explore RAW's impact on the world stage, the challenges it faces in an ever-evolving landscape, and the heroes who remain steadfast in their commitment to safeguarding humanity.

## Chapter 9: The Silent Watchers - Intelligence Analysis and Strategic Assessments

In the labyrinthine world of intelligence, the task of making sense of vast amounts of information falls to the silent watchers—the intelligence analysts who sift through the noise, connect the fragments, and distill critical insights that guide the decision-making process. This chapter explores the indispensable role of intelligence analysis and strategic assessments within RAW, revealing the hidden work behind the scenes.

Intelligence analysts form the backbone of RAW's operations, working diligently to transform raw data into actionable intelligence. They meticulously gather, evaluate, and synthesize information from a myriad of sources, ranging from human intelligence reports to intercepted communications, satellite imagery, and open-source data. Their expertise lies not only in deciphering the information but also in identifying patterns, discerning hidden connections, and predicting future developments.

Within the confines of intelligence analysis, analysts are tasked with piecing together the puzzle of global events, providing insights into geopolitical dynamics, and identifying emerging threats. Their work extends beyond the immediate scope of operations, as they are responsible for crafting long-term strategic assessments that inform national policies and help shape India's foreign relations.

Intelligence analysts employ a range of analytical techniques and methodologies, combining rigorous research, critical thinking, and domain expertise to derive accurate and timely assessments. They scrutinize the intentions and capabilities of foreign entities, analyze geopolitical trends, and evaluate the impact of global developments on India's national security interests.

Strategic assessments crafted by RAW's analysts are instrumental in providing policymakers with a comprehensive understanding of the complex world in which they operate. These assessments enable informed decision-making, allowing policymakers to anticipate challenges, identify opportunities, and develop strategies to safeguard India's interests.

However, the work of intelligence analysts is not without its challenges. They operate in an environment characterized by incomplete information, misinformation, and rapidly evolving threats. Analysts must navigate through ambiguity, assess the reliability of sources, and discern the accuracy and relevance of the information at hand. Their work requires intellectual rigor, objectivity, and the ability to think critically amidst the fog of uncertainty.

Chapter 9 of "Unseen Shadows: Inside the Realm of RAW" unveils the crucial role played by intelligence analysis and strategic assessments within the agency. It highlights the tireless work of these silent watchers, who remain dedicated to uncovering the truth, deciphering complex landscapes, and providing invaluable insights that inform critical decisions.

Join us as we delve into the world of intelligence analysis, where the silent watchers toil behind the scenes, shaping the course of events with their intellect and expertise. In the upcoming chapters, we will continue to explore the multifaceted realm of intelligence analysis, examine its impact on RAW's operations, and shed light on the dedicated individuals who are the backbone of RAW's analytical capabilities.

## Chapter 10: The Ethical Quandaries - Balancing Secrecy and Accountability

The world of intelligence agencies exists in a realm cloaked in secrecy, where operations are shrouded and the need to protect national security reigns supreme. However, within this realm, ethical quandaries arise, testing the delicate balance between maintaining secrecy and upholding democratic values. In this chapter, we explore the ethical challenges faced by RAW as it grapples with the imperative of secrecy, the necessity of accountability, and the delicate dance between the two.

RAW's mandate demands a high level of secrecy to effectively carry out its operations. The clandestine nature of its work necessitates the protection of sources, methods, and sensitive information. This culture of secrecy is crucial for preserving the integrity of intelligence operations, ensuring the safety of operatives, and preventing adversaries from gaining insights into RAW's capabilities.

However, maintaining secrecy raises ethical questions. In a democratic society, transparency and accountability are fundamental pillars of governance. Balancing the need for secrecy with the imperative of accountability can be a challenging task. RAW must navigate a complex terrain, where it must be answerable to the democratic principles upon which the nation is built, while safeguarding sensitive information that could compromise national security if disclosed.

The challenge lies in establishing mechanisms that ensure oversight and accountability without jeopardizing the effectiveness of intelligence operations. RAW operates within a legal framework that outlines its mandate, but the specific details of its operations remain shielded from public scrutiny. This limited transparency raises questions about checks and balances, the potential for abuse of power, and the scope for external oversight.

RAW addresses these ethical quandaries by adhering to a system of internal oversight mechanisms. The agency has dedicated review boards, composed of senior officials and experts, tasked with assessing the legality, appropriateness, and ethical implications of its operations. These boards provide an internal check on RAW's activities, ensuring compliance with legal and ethical standards.

Additionally, RAW operates within the larger framework of democratic institutions, collaborating with the executive, legislature, and judiciary to strike a balance between secrecy and accountability. The agency cooperates with oversight committees, providing necessary information and insights to elected representatives responsible for ensuring oversight of intelligence activities.

However, the tension between secrecy and accountability remains an ongoing challenge. Striking the right balance requires continuous evaluation, adaptation, and a commitment to upholding democratic principles. RAW recognizes the importance of maintaining public trust while protecting sensitive information, and it remains dedicated to fostering a system that fosters transparency, accountability, and democratic values within the bounds of national security imperatives.

Chapter 10 of "Unseen Shadows: Inside the Realm of RAW" delves into the ethical quandaries that RAW faces in its pursuit of national security. It sheds light on the delicate dance between secrecy and accountability, the mechanisms in place to ensure oversight, and the ongoing efforts to strike a balance that upholds democratic values while protecting the nation's interests.

Join us as we explore the ethical dimensions of intelligence work, where the imperative of secrecy collides with the need for accountability, and where RAW strives to uphold democratic principles while safeguarding the nation from threats that lurk in the shadows. In the upcoming chapters, we will continue to unravel the ethical complexities of RAW's operations, shedding light on the agency's commitment to responsible governance, transparency, and the preservation of democratic values.

## Chapter 11: Adversaries Unveiled - Emerging Threats in a Changing World

The world is in a constant state of flux, with emerging threats and evolving challenges reshaping the global security landscape. In this chapter, we delve into the adversaries that have unveiled themselves before RAW, posing new challenges and necessitating adaptive strategies. We explore the shifting dynamics of global security, technological advancements, and the agency's response to safeguarding India's interests in this ever-changing world.

One of the significant emerging threats that RAW faces is the rise of cyber warfare. As technology becomes increasingly intertwined with all aspects of society, the potential for cyber attacks on critical infrastructure, government systems, and even individuals grows exponentially. RAW's focus on bolstering its cyber intelligence capabilities enables it to detect and counter cyber threats, safeguarding India's digital infrastructure and national security.

Another emerging challenge lies in the realm of hybrid warfare, where adversaries employ a combination of conventional and unconventional tactics to achieve their objectives. These tactics include disinformation campaigns, propaganda, economic coercion, and non-state actors operating as proxies. RAW's intelligence apparatus remains vigilant in monitoring and countering these multifaceted threats, working closely with partner agencies to expose and neutralize attempts to undermine India's security and interests.

The global arena has also witnessed the resurgence of regional conflicts and the rise of non-state actors with transnational ambitions. RAW remains at the forefront in monitoring these complex dynamics, gathering intelligence on shifting alliances, proxy wars, and the exploitation of fragile states. Its expertise in understanding regional dynamics and cultural nuances allows it to anticipate emerging threats and develop strategies to counteract them effectively.

Moreover, RAW confronts the challenges posed by emerging technologies, such as artificial intelligence, autonomous systems, and biotechnology. These advancements offer both opportunities and risks, as they can be harnessed for various purposes, including warfare, espionage, and the manipulation of information. RAW stays abreast of these technological developments, understanding their implications and working to harness them to its advantage while mitigating the associated risks.

Climate change and resource scarcity also emerge as pressing challenges with far-reaching security implications. RAW recognizes the need to incorporate environmental factors into its threat assessments, understanding the potential for conflicts over scarce resources, displacement of populations, and the exacerbation of existing tensions. The agency works in collaboration with environmental experts, providing critical intelligence to policymakers to address these challenges and foster sustainable security solutions.

Chapter 11 of "Unseen Shadows: Inside the Realm of RAW" reveals the ever-shifting landscape of global security, where emerging threats demand proactive responses. RAW's ability to adapt to these challenges, harness new technologies, and anticipate future developments ensures its effectiveness in protecting India's interests. The agency remains agile, continuously monitoring and analyzing the emerging adversaries that pose risks to the nation's security and prosperity.

Join us as we delve into the world of emerging threats, where the adversaries that RAW confronts are ever-evolving, and the agency's response is marked by innovation, adaptability, and a commitment to safeguarding India's interests in a changing world. In the forthcoming chapters, we will explore the strategies employed by RAW to counter these threats, the collaborations forged with international partners, and the continuous pursuit of staying one step ahead of the adversaries.

# Chapter 12: Legacy of Excellence - Shaping the Future of RAW

The legacy of RAW is one of excellence, dedication, and an unwavering commitment to safeguarding India's interests. As we conclude our exploration of the realm of RAW, this final chapter serves as a reflection on the agency's enduring impact and its ongoing efforts to shape the future of intelligence.

Throughout its history, RAW has left an indelible mark on India's national security landscape. From its early days as a fledgling intelligence agency to its current position as a formidable force, RAW's operations have contributed to the protection of India's sovereignty, the preservation of democracy, and the safeguarding of its people.

The agency's successes in counterterrorism, counterproliferation, and countering hybrid threats have earned it a reputation as a key player in the global intelligence community. RAW's collaborations with international partners, its cutting-edge technological capabilities, and its commitment to excellence have placed it at the forefront of intelligence operations.

However, the challenges facing RAW persist and continue to evolve. The nature of threats, the advancements in technology, and the shifting dynamics of global security demand that the agency remain vigilant, adaptable, and forward-thinking. RAW recognizes the need for continuous innovation, investment in technology and human capital, and the cultivation of strategic partnerships to effectively counter emerging challenges.

One key area of focus for RAW's future is harnessing the power of artificial intelligence and big data analytics. The agency recognizes the potential of these technologies in processing vast amounts of information, identifying patterns, and deriving actionable intelligence. By leveraging these capabilities, RAW aims to enhance its situational awareness, improve decision-making processes, and stay ahead of emerging threats.

Additionally, RAW remains committed to nurturing a diverse and skilled workforce. The agency understands the importance of recruiting and retaining talent from diverse backgrounds, fostering creativity, and embracing different perspectives. This inclusivity strengthens its analytical capabilities, enhances its understanding of complex global dynamics, and ensures the agency's continued relevance in a rapidly changing world.

Furthermore, RAW is conscious of the need for robust oversight mechanisms and ethical governance. The agency recognizes that maintaining public trust and adhering to democratic principles are vital in preserving its legitimacy and effectiveness. It strives to strike the delicate balance between safeguarding national security and upholding the values of transparency, accountability, and respect for human rights.

Chapter 12 of "Unseen Shadows: Inside the Realm of RAW" concludes our exploration of this storied intelligence agency. It is a testament to RAW's legacy of excellence, its contributions to India's security, and its ongoing efforts to shape the future of intelligence. RAW's commitment to adapting to emerging challenges, fostering innovation, and upholding democratic values ensures its relevance in an ever-evolving world.

Join us as we bid farewell to this remarkable journey, recognizing the dedication of RAW's operatives, the complexity of their work, and the lasting impact they have on the security and well-being of the nation. As RAW continues its mission, we look forward to witnessing the agency's continued excellence and its unwavering commitment to safeguarding India's interests in the years to come.